YOU CAN USE MONEY WISELY

SPEND OR SAVE?

You Choose the Ending

by Connie Colwell Miller • illustrated by Victoria Assanelli

Do you ever wish you could change a story or choose a different ending?

IN THESE BOOKS, YOU CAN!

Read along and when you see this:

WHAT HAPPENS NEXT?

Skip to the page for that choice, and see what happens.

In this story, Miles earns money from pet sitting. Will he save it, or will he spend it? YOU make the choices!

Miles earned $30 pet sitting. He really wants to buy a new video game that all his friends are playing. At the store, Miles sees some trading cards he wants.

WHAT HAPPENS NEXT?

→ If Miles buys the cards, turn the page.

If Miles saves his money for the video game, turn to page 20. ←

3

Miles buys the trading cards. They cost $4. That leaves him with $26.

Miles and Mom go to a department store next. Miles sees a T-shirt that he likes. "That's super cool!" Miles says. "Can I buy it?"

Mom replies, "It's your choice."

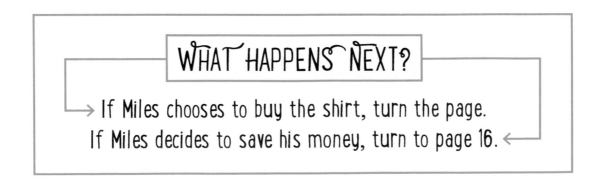

WHAT HAPPENS NEXT?

→ If Miles chooses to buy the shirt, turn the page.
If Miles decides to save his money, turn to page 16. ←

Miles buys the shirt. It costs $10. Now he only has
$16 left. Mom stops at the gas station. In the store,
Miles sees his favorite candy.

WHAT HAPPENS NEXT?

→ If Miles buys the candy, too, turn the page.
If Miles saves his money, turn to page 14. ←

"Mom!" Miles says. "They have Gooey Yum-Yums here!" Miles buys the candy and eats it in the car.

TURN THE PAGE →

At the video game store, Miles finds the game he wanted.
It is on sale for $45. But he only has $15 left.

"Mom," Miles asks, "Will you give me $30 so I can buy this game? All my friends are playing it! Please??"

TURN THE PAGE →

"I'm sorry, Miles," she says. "I have bills to pay this week, so I can't afford $30 right now. You'll have to save up for it."

Miles is disappointed that he can't get the game. He should have saved his money instead of spending it on other things.

THE END

Go to page 23.

Miles doesn't buy the candy. At the video game store, Miles sees the game is on sale for $45. He only has $16 left, so he can't buy the game today.

Mom says, "We will have to come back after you earn more money." Now Miles has to wait to enjoy the new game.

THE END

→ Go to page 23. ←

Miles wants to buy the T-shirt. But he decides to save his money for the video game he really wants.

At the video game store, the game is on sale for $45, but Miles only has $26. "Mom, will you help me pay for the game?" Miles asks.

TURN THE PAGE →

Since Miles saved most of his money, Mom agrees to help. She says, "I will loan you the money, but you need to do chores this weekend before you can play it."

Miles gets the game, but he spends the weekend doing chores to pay back his mom. When he's done, he gets to play the game.

THE END

Go to page 23.

Miles saves his money. He really wants the new video game, and he has more pet sitting jobs coming up. Miles sees other items he would like, but he saves his money for the game.

One week later, Miles has earned $20 more from pet sitting. He has saved $50 total. Great news! The video game is on sale for $45. Miles has enough to buy it!

TURN THE PAGE →

Miles is glad he saved his money. Now he enjoys playing his new video game with his friends!

THE END

THINK AGAIN

- What happened at the end of the path you chose?
- Did you like that ending?
- Go back to page 3. Read the story again and pick different choices. How did the story change?

We all have to make choices about how to spend our money. If you wanted something expensive, would you save up for it? Or would you spend your money on other things?

To Miles, my saver.—C.C.M.

AMICUS ILLUSTRATED and AMICUS INK
are published by Amicus
P.O. Box 227, Mankato, MN 56002.
www.amicuspublishing.us

Library of Congress Cataloging-in-Publication Data
Names: Miller, Connie Colwell, 1976- author. | Assanelli, Victoria, 1984- illustrator. | Miller, Connie Colwell, 1976- Making good choices. | Amicus Illustrated. | Amicus (Firm : Mankato, Minn.)
Title: You can use money wisely: spend or save? / by Connie Colwell Miller ; illustrated by Victoria Assanelli.
Description: Mankato, Minnesota : Amicus, 2021. | Series: Amicus illustrated | Audience: Ages 6-9 years | Audience: Grades 2-3 | Summary: "In this illustrated choose-your-own-ending picture book, Miles must choose between spending his hard-earned money on small items right away and saving up for a more expensive video game that he really wants. Readers make choices for Miles and read what happens next, with each story path leading to different consequences. Includes four different endings and discussion questions"—Provided by publisher.
Identifiers: LCCN 2019045986 (print) | LCCN 2019045987 (ebook) | ISBN 9781681519883 (Library Binding) | ISBN 9781681526355 (Paperback) | ISBN 9781645490739 (PDF)
Subjects: LCSH: Money. | Plot-your-own stories. | Illustrated children's books. | Readers.
Classification: LCC GN450.59 .M55 2021 (print) | LCC GN450.59 (ebook) | DDC 332.4--dc23
LC record available at https://lccn.loc.gov/2019045986
LC ebook record available at https://lccn.loc.gov/2019045987

Editor: Rebecca Glaser
Series Designer: Kathleen Petelinsek
Book Designer: Aubrey Harper

ABOUT THE AUTHOR

Connie Colwell Miller is a writer, editor, and instructor who lives in southern Minnesota with her four children. She has written over 100 books for young children. She likes to tell stories to her kids to teach them important life lessons.

ABOUT THE ILLUSTRATOR

Victoria Assanelli was born during the autumn of 1984 in Buenos Aires, Argentina. She spent most of her childhood playing with her grandparents, reading books, and drawing doodles. She began working as an illustrator in 2007 and has illustrated several textbooks and storybooks since then.